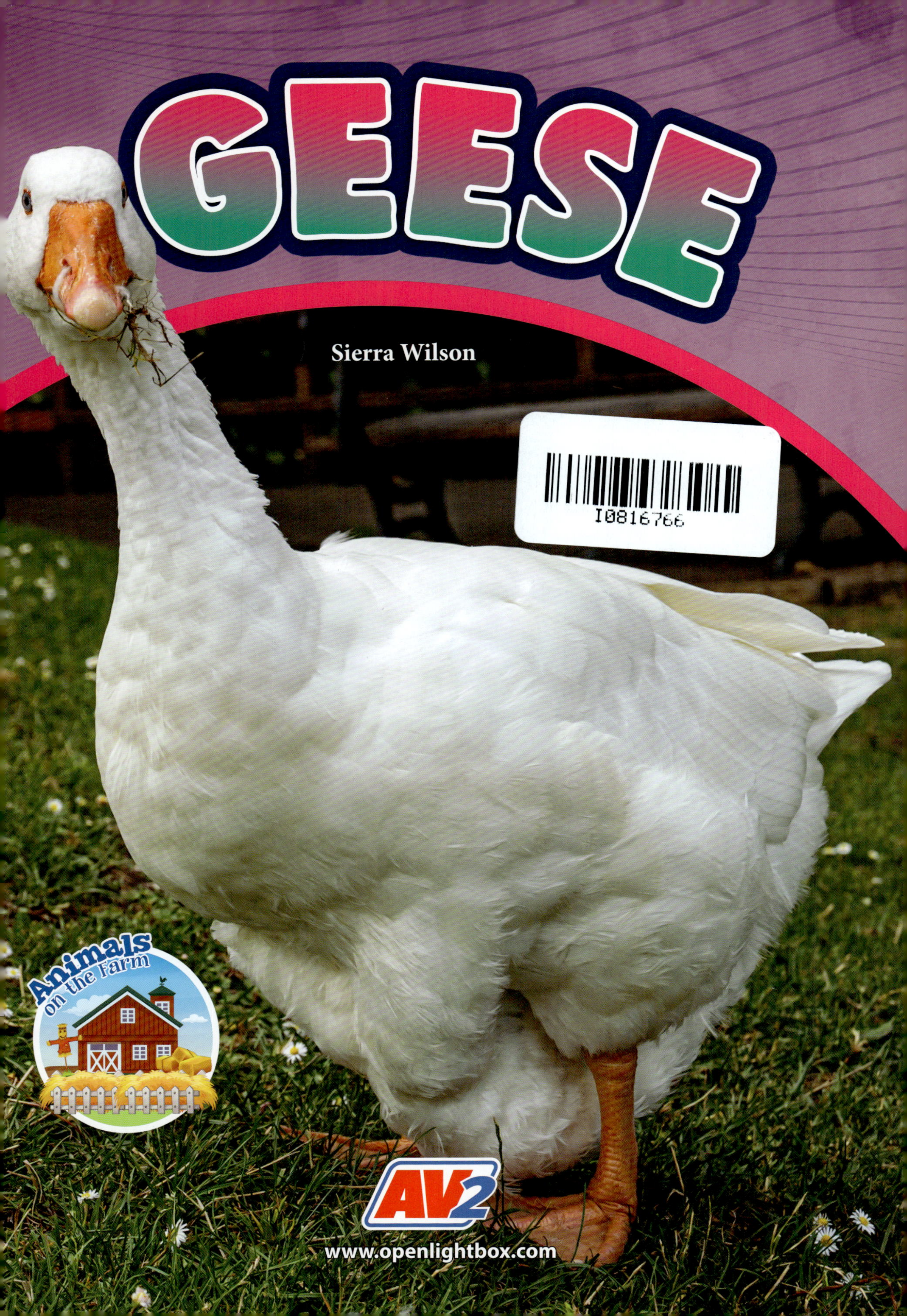

GEESE
Sierra Wilson
I0816766
Animals on the Farm
AV2
www.openlightbox.com

Step 1
Go to **www.openlightbox.com**

Step 2
Enter this unique code

XUMSOQLDF

Step 3
Explore your interactive eBook!

AV2 is optimized for use on any device

Your interactive eBook comes with...

Contents
Browse a live contents page to easily navigate through resources

Audio
Listen to sections of the book read aloud

Videos
Watch informative video clips

Weblinks
Gain additional information for research

Slideshows
View images and captions

Try This!
Complete activities and hands-on experiments

Key Words
Study vocabulary, and complete a matching word activity

Quizzes
Test your knowledge

Share
Share titles within your Learning Management System (LMS) or Library Circulation System

Citation
Create bibliographical references following APA, CMOS, and MLA styles

This title is part of our AV2 digital subscription

1-Year Grades K–5 Subscription
ISBN 978-1-7911-3320-7

Access hundreds of AV2 titles with our digital subscription.
Sign up for a FREE trial at **www.openlightbox.com/trial**

GEESE

CONTENTS

Geese are **waterfowl**. They belong to the **family** *Anatidae*, which also includes ducks and swans. All of the birds in this family have webbed feet and live on or near water.

Some farmers raise geese for food or feathers. Others use geese to control weeds. Some geese even act as guards. This is because geese are known for their loud honks. They often use these honks to warn other geese about possible threats.

Geese are sometimes seen as aggressive. However, these birds are just protective of their territory and family. They are intelligent and brave animals that play an important role on many farms.

Goose or Swan

Goose		Swan
Short, thick neck	vs.	Long, thin neck
Light and small	vs.	Heavy and tall
Short **wingspan**	vs.	Long wingspan
White, black, gray, or brown feathers	vs.	White or black feathers

The *Anatidae* family includes almost 200 different types of birds.

All about Geese

Geese are social birds. In nature, they live in large groups. Some **species** of goose have groups that reach up to 100 members. Geese on the farm also like to live together.

There are several **domestic** goose **breeds**. These breeds have been developed by farmers to grow very large. Due to their size, most domestic geese cannot fly.

Unlike domestic geese, wild geese are well-known for their ability to fly long distances. Some wild geese **migrate** during winter. Every year, they fly more than 2,000 miles (3,200 kilometers) to reach warm areas.

Most wild goose flocks fly in a V-shaped formation.

Domestic Goose Breeds

American Buff

- Produces up to 25 eggs a year
- Friendly and gentle
- Light brown feathers

Chinese

- Produces 30 to 50 eggs a year
- Good at controlling weeds
- White or brown feathers with a large head knob

Embden

- Produces 15 to 30 eggs a year
- Raised mostly for meat
- White feathers

Roman

- Produces 25 to 35 eggs a year
- Calm and friendly
- White feathers with a tuft on its head

Sebastopol

- Produces 25 to 35 eggs a year
- Raised as a show goose
- Curled white feathers

Toulouse

- Produces 25 to 50 eggs a year
- Large in size
- Gray feathers

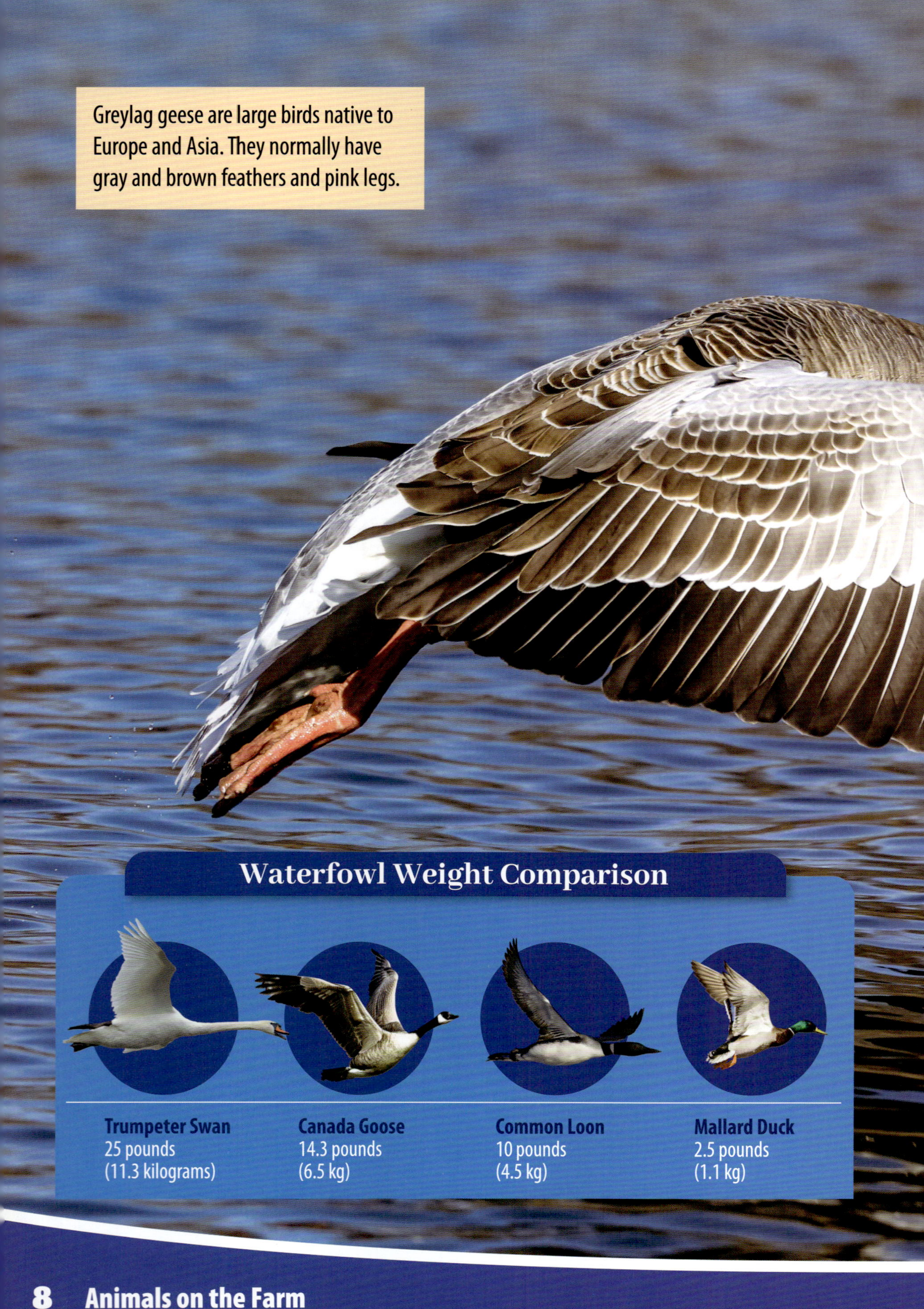

Greylag geese are large birds native to Europe and Asia. They normally have gray and brown feathers and pink legs.

Waterfowl Weight Comparison

Trumpeter Swan	Canada Goose	Common Loon	Mallard Duck
25 pounds (11.3 kilograms)	14.3 pounds (6.5 kg)	10 pounds (4.5 kg)	2.5 pounds (1.1 kg)

Goose History

Humans have been domesticating geese for many years. Geese may have first been raised by humans in China as early as 7,000 years ago. Domestic geese were also kept by farmers in ancient Egypt and Europe. People raised geese for their eggs and meat. They also collected goose feathers to make warm pillows, quilts, and coats.

Most modern goose breeds come from two species of wild goose. These are the Greylag goose and the swan goose. People focused on developing breeds that could lay more eggs.

Goose Shelter

Geese like to wander and need space to explore. However, they also need protection from **predators**. This is why they should be kept in an enclosure or fenced field.

Geese also need a shelter to use at night. Unlike other farm birds, they do not need nesting boxes or **roosts** in their indoor shelter. Instead, they need fresh, clean bedding materials such as pine shavings, straw, or peat moss. Their shelter should be secure, without any holes and a latching door to help keep them safe from predators.

Foxes, coyotes, and wolves are some of the predators that might attack both wild and domestic geese.

Fascinating Facts

There are **more than 20 goose species** in the world.

Goose Features

Geese look like large ducks with longer necks. They can be many colors, including gray, brown, and white. Geese may have a wingspan of up to 6 feet (1.8 m).

Like other waterfowl, geese have three types of feathers. Short, fluffy feathers call down help geese keep warm. Contour feathers form a layer above the down. They lock together to keep out wind and water. Strong feathers on the wings, called flight feathers, help geese fly. Even geese that cannot fly have flight feathers.

Legs

Goose legs are positioned close to the front of the bird's body. This makes geese better at walking than ducks or swans.

Feet

Geese have large, webbed feet to swim.

Bill

Geese have orange or black bills that are sometimes humped at the top. The tips of goose bills are slightly curved to help the birds grip the grass they eat.

Body

Goose bodies are large, round, and covered with feathers. Domestic geese have more fat on their bodies than wild geese.

What Do Geese Eat?

Geese are omnivores. This means that they can eat both plants and animals. However, one of their favorite foods is grass. Grassy plants often make up most of their diet. In fact, geese can be used as natural lawnmowers, as long as the plants they eat have not been sprayed with **pesticides**. Some farms use geese to weed around crops such as corn, strawberries, and fruit trees.

Along with grass, geese can also be fed goose feed purchased from a store. For treats, geese enjoy peas, chopped grapes, berries, and broccoli. Geese also need access to small rocks and pebbles, called grit, which they will swallow. The grit will stay in a goose's **gizzard** to help grind up food and make it more **digestible**.

About 1 acre (0.4 hectares) of land can provide enough food for 20 to 40 geese.

Fascinating Facts

A goose egg can be up to **three times larger** than a chicken egg.

Goose Life Cycle

A male goose is called a gander. A female goose is called a hen or simply a goose. Young geese are known as goslings.

Geese only lay eggs from February to July each year. Domestic geese can lay up to 50 eggs per year. Depending on the species, wild geese only lay about 5 to 12 eggs a year. Most geese **mate** for life. However, some domestic geese might find different partners every year.

Egg

Eggs must be kept warm by their parents or in an **incubator** in order to hatch. Goose eggs hatch about 30 days after being laid.

Gosling

Goslings can eat and swim on their own the same day they hatch. They stay close to their parents for safety. Goslings have soft, downy feathers. They develop flight feathers when they are about 2 to 3 months old.

Adult

Geese are ready to mate at about 2 years of age. Ganders and hens are highly protective of their families. They will hiss at anything that comes near their goslings. Domestic geese can live up to about 20 years.

Caring for Geese

Along with safe shelter and food, geese need access to plenty of water. A pond or large tub of clean water will meet their needs. Geese use water for both drinking and bathing.

Geese need companionship to live a happy life. A goose can be part of a mixed group with ducks and chickens. However, this mixed group should include at least one other goose.

If properly cared for, geese are usually strong and healthy. **Veterinarians** can give recommendations about the best foods for different geese. They can also help when geese show signs of illness.

Some geese are kept as pets. They can develop strong bonds with their humans and the other pets in a household.

Myths and Legends

Geese are found all around the world, and so are stories about them. According to an ancient Egyptian legend, the Sun was hatched from an egg laid by the goose-god Geb. In ancient Rome, geese were considered sacred to the goddess Juno.

In Asia, the Hindu creator god, Brahma, was sometimes depicted as riding a giant goose. Folk tales about geese are also popular in many other cultures.

According to Roman writer Livy, a flock of geese lived inside Juno's temple in Rome. In 390 BC, the geese saved the city from an enemy attack by hissing and flapping their wings to alert people of the danger.

Raven and Goose Wife

Every year, wild geese migrate great distances. This is a native Alaskan story about a raven who fell in love with a migrating goose.

Long ago, Raven fell in love with a beautiful goose. They had a wonderful summer together, but in the fall the goose said she needed to fly south with the other geese. Snow was coming soon. Raven loved his goose companion so much that he decided to migrate with her. Raven was a strong flier, but he soon became tired. The goose tried to carry him, but he was too heavy. Next, her family tried to carry him, but they became tired, too. Finally, the goose's father told Raven that they still had far to go and would not be able to carry him. Raven was sad, but he saw the wisdom in the goose father's words. He returned home, and this is why ravens do not migrate to this day.

Goose Quiz

1 How long do domestic geese live?

2 How many eggs can a Toulouse goose lay per year?

3 How much does a Canada goose weigh?

4 How many different species of goose are there in the world?

5 Which part of a goose's body contains small rocks and pebbles to grind up food?

6 What is a baby goose called?

7 Which goose feathers are short, fluffy, and used for warmth?

8 Whom should a goose see if it shows signs of an illness?

ANSWERS: 1. Up to about 20 years **2.** 25 to 50 **3.** 14.3 pounds (6.5 kg) **4.** More than 20 **5.** The gizzard **6.** A gosling **7.** Down **8.** A veterinarian

Key Words

breeds: groups of animals of the same species with similar characteristics and family history

digestible: capable of being broken down within the body

domestic: tamed and kept by humans

family: a group of living things belonging to different species that share certain characteristics

gizzard: a strong, muscular pouch that forms part of a bird's stomach

incubator: a machine used to keep eggs at a specific temperature

mate: form a pair and produce offspring

migrate: to travel to locations based on the season

pesticides: substances used to kill or control insects and other organisms that harm crops

predators: animals that hunt and eat other animals

roosts: bars or other perches for birds to sit on above the ground

species: a group of closely related animals or plants

veterinarians: animal doctors

waterfowl: birds that spend much of their life in or around water

wingspan: the maximum width of a set of wings, measured from tip to tip

Index

Get the best of both worlds.

AV2 bridges the gap between print and digital.

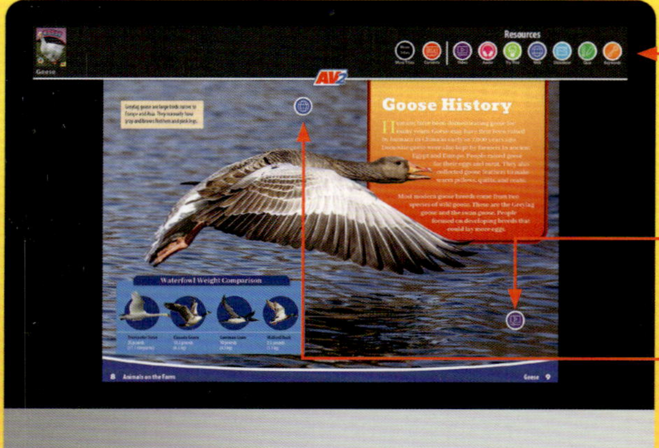

The expandable resources toolbar enables quick access to content including **videos**, **audio**, **activities**, **weblinks**, **slideshows**, **quizzes**, and **key words**.

Animated videos make static images come alive.

Resource icons on each page help readers to further **explore key concepts**.

Published by Lightbox Learning Inc.
276 5th Avenue
Suite 704 #917
New York, NY 10001
Website: www.openlightbox.com

Library of Congress Control Number: 2022947280

ISBN 978-1-7911-4760-0 (hardcover)
ISBN 978-1-7911-4761-7 (softcover)
ISBN 978-1-7911-4762-4 (multi-user eBook)

Printed in Guangzhou, China
1 2 3 4 5 6 7 8 9 0 26 25 24 23 22

122022
101121

Project Coordinator: Sara Cucini
Designer: Jean Faye Marie Rodriguez

Photo Credits
Every reasonable effort has been made to trace ownership and to obtain permission to reprint copyright material. The publisher would be pleased to have any errors or omissions brought to its attention so that they may be corrected in subsequent printings. The publisher acknowledges Alamy, Getty Images, Minden Pictures, and Shutterstock as its primary image suppliers for this title.